CO-OPERATIVES IN AMERICA
Their Past, Present, and Future

Special Edition

PRINTED FOR

THE CO-OPERATIVE LEAGUE

OF THE U. S. A.

Co-operatives
IN AMERICA
Their Past, Present and Future

BY *Ellis Cowling*

WITH AN INTRODUCTION BY

J. P. WARBASSE

President of the Co-operative League of the U. S. A.

COWARD-McCANN, INC.

New York 1938

THIRD IMPRESSION

MANUFACTURED IN THE UNITED STATES OF AMERICA

BY THE VAN REES PRESS · NEW YORK

This book is dedicated to Marion Brevier Cowling who helped her husband in every step of its preparation.

Acknowledgments

THE completion of this work would have been impossible without the help of friends.

I am indebted to the directors and manager of the Trumbull Farm Bureau Co-operative of Cortland, Ohio, for allowing me time enough from my regular duties to complete the writing.

Mr. A. W. Ricker, editor of the *Farmers Union Herald,* Mr. Thomas Cheek of the Oklahoma Farmers Union, Mr. L. S. Herron, editor of the *Nebraska Union Farmer,* Mr. Chester Graham of the Michigan Farmers Union, and especially Mrs. Gladys Talbott Edwards, Junior Leader of the National Farmers Union, gave invaluable aid in collecting material about Farmers Union Co-operatives.

Mr. Merlin Miller of the Consumers Co-operative Association of North Kansas City rendered a like service in providing information about the organization with which he is identified.

Dr. James Peter Warbasse of the Co-operative League of the U. S. A. and Mr. A. W. Warinner of the Central States Co-operative League loaned me valuable historical material on the American co-operative movement.

ACKNOWLEDGMENTS

I am grateful to Dr. David Sonquist of the Central States Co-operative League, to Mr. Anthony Lehner of the Pennsylvania Farm Bureau Co-operative Association, to Mr. Thomas Coward and his editorial staff for reading the manuscript and making many helpful suggestions for its improvement.

ELLIS COWLING

Introduction

Co-operation in America is not new. It began among the animals that practiced mutual aid in their economic and social lives—in getting their food, and in protecting themselves from the elements and from their enemies. It continued among the primitive peoples of this continent, who did the same things in their different ways. The North American Indians organized themselves co-operatively and carried on their affairs in closer conformity to what are now called Rochdale methods than do many societies which are called co-operative today.

The Indians set up a tribal democracy in which each invested, as his contribution to share capital, his goods and his man power. They distributed to each member according to his needs. From distribution they moved back toward production. The chase, the forests, and the fields yielded food which was co-operatively apportioned. Each member got what he required and what in man power he paid for. No funds received interest, because no money was needed. The use of wampum was exceptional, and unnecessary within the tribe. Reserves, as a common surplus saving in the form of food, clothing, and other supplies, were built up to carry the tribe through the winter or other difficult season. The important fact was that all production and distribution were for service and not for private profit. Industry was not to make the difference between the cost and selling price by selling to somebody else.

In the strict meaning of the word this could not be called Rochdale co-operation. It was long before the Rochdale period. But it was the form of collectivism out of which Rochdale co-operation grew.

Were the high ethical standards of these people the result of these co-operative practices or did they practice co-operation because of their standards of ethics? Perhaps the latter is the case, and perhaps they employed the methods that are most natural. Certainly the co-operation of the Indians was most conducive to their preservation and survival. But when the white man with his individualistic, competitive, and acquisitive methods overwhelmed the Indians and coveted their property, he attempted to compel the Indians to adopt his ways. The Indians usually observed treaties; the white man broke them. When the Government put the Indians on isolated tribal lands, they continued with their co-operative methods and administered together their pooled possessions. Then followed a violation of their co-operative practices committed by the United States Government. An act was passed forbidding collective methods and compelling the splitting up of tribal property into small holdings for the individual Indians. Each Indian was made by law to own personally an individual piece of land. This was done at the behest of real estate speculators, white frontiersmen, and companies who desired to get the lands from the Indians. It was impossible to acquire the lands from the Indians while they were jointly held. But when each shareholder was compelled by law to take back his land capital into his own hands and its joint administration was broken up, the lone Indian was left at the mercy of unscrupulous forces which with the help of the Government, had little difficulty in robbing him of his property.

Now a new development is in process. The present Federal Government has appointed an Indian commissioner who not only knows the ethnology of the Indians but who understands co-operation also. Measures are on foot to restore to the Indians their ancient right to carry on their affairs co-operatively; they are also being taught the modern Rochdale methods and are being encouraged to apply these methods to their economic affairs. Honorable amends at last are offered for an old wrong.

The Mormons, when they settled in Utah, got from some source the collectivist idea. They organized and maintained a multitude of collective institutions which were co-operative in nature. They had a federation of their supply societies, which conducted a wholesale with a great warehouse in Salt

Lake City. This idea they probably acquired from the Indians and out of their own natural impulses as they strove for an ideal. Their co-operation was destroyed by their cupidity. When the possibilities of wealth and individual acquisitiveness were seen, the Mormons dropped their co-operative practices to give each individual the chance to acquire what he could. Some relics of the old co-operative tendency still survive, but in general this cult has committed itself to the profit economy of scarcity and individualistic acquisition. This means that a few are rich, but most are poor.

The many collectivist colonies that have developed in America also have exemplified some aspects of co-operation. The Shakers, dating back to 1787, practiced co-operative purchasing although they were essentially a productive and marketing enterprise. But they, like their many successors, had first in mind the consumers' philosophy. They were originally organized to be self-sufficient. They planned to produce most or all of the things they needed to consume. This is a fundamental concept of consumers' co-operation. Modern co-operation learns how to distribute first. But its members have capital which they have earned outside of the co-operative movement. The colonists had no other employment. They went to work together. They produced co-operatively together. They distributed co-operatively among themselves the products of their labor. They were co-operative consumers in the highest sense of the word. They neither bought nor sold for profit.

This was their ideal. But it was only an ideal. It lasted only during an initial stage. In time they found that they could produce more than they could consume. They sold the surplus. They made money. They got rich. They contracted the qualities of the capitalistic society by which they were surrounded. They caught the contagion from the very world from which they had hoped to escape. In the end, they divided their property among the individuals, and what was once an ideal and a successful business scheme came to an end. This has happened to a multitude of "co-operative colonies" which were set up in the United States during the first half of the past century. They are gone, with only their experience left to teach its lesson to those who may learn.

Among these colonies were New Lanark, the Amana Society, the Harmonists, the Bethel Commune, Brook Farm, and a hundred more—all ended largely because they departed from pure consumers' co-operation and went into profit business as marketing associations. There still survive a few old colonies practicing co-operation; but they are religious organizations and the members are held together by religious zeal. Such a one is the Huterisch Colony which adheres to the primitive Christianity. The few existing new colonies are apparently weak and temporary.

The American movement should have learned its lesson in the school of experience. It has made mistakes in some fields and it has been wisely guided in others. Co-operative societies in other countries likewise have suffered their mistakes. British co-operation has grown in a soil fertilized by as many casualities as occurred in America. But as serious and as costly as these experiences have been, they have been vastly less than the failures in profit business; and they continue to be less.

One co-operative principle has been generally observed in this country during the past twenty years. That is the principle of neutrality. American societies remain neutral in questions of politics and religion. They have no sides in politics nor do they endorse political candidates. As a result, the movement has not been split. American societies have on their boards of directors people of varying religious affiliations, people of all the leading political parties, and people of no religion and of no politics. In America, co-operation lives up to the highest co-operative possibilities in providing a common ground upon which all people may unite in harmony. American societies find strength in their neutrality.

This book which Mr. Cowling has written tells the story of co-operation in this country from about the Rochdale period. It begins with an honest recital of the mistakes and failures of the early movement. Bungling, errors, and failure in the early days were the rule. It might seem that co-operation had suffered staggering blows from which it could not recover. The setbacks might seem to represent irretrievable loss. But this is not the case. Every error taught its lesson. Co-operation, developing in the midst of a profit economy, is experimental. The American pioneers went to the school of trial and error. We now know their mistakes. We know how to avoid them. The pioneers paid the price; we are reaping the advantage.

In our American soil, fertilized by the blood and the dead bodies of a thousand societies, is now growing a movement enriched and nourished by the experiences of the past. We should not blame these pioneers. We owe them our gratitude and homage. They had little to guide them; we have much.

This book is a fair and clear picture also of the success into which American co-operation is growing. It is factual, and its philosophy is sound. It is a help to the understanding of this expanding movement, which on the whole is still much misunderstood. Those who entertain the idea that labor, organized as producers, can solve the problems of society, or even the problems of the working class, need the enlightenment which this book provides. The new economics is under obligations to Mr. Cowling for this lucid exposition of the co-operative method of business, now well advanced in America.

J. P. WARBASSE.

Contents

CO-OPERATIVES IN AMERICA
Their Past, Present, and Future

CHAPTER I

Three Englishmen
Upset a World

CHANGE IS IN THE SADDLE. No one can look at the past decade of American life and not be impressed with that fact. The years previous to 1929 saw the nation's business spiraling to the peak of a dizzy paper prosperity. Men talked of a new era when poverty would be abolished forever. The Republicanism of Coolidge and Mellon was looked upon as the last word in government. Here and there voices did speak of growing insecurity among laborers and increasing farm tenancy. But no one listened. The ears of the nation were tuned to other things.

Then the stock market crashed. The price of securities hit a toboggan. Business activity followed. The great productive and distributive machinery of America slowed down. Millions lost their jobs virtually over night. Want stalked a land whose citizens prated about overproduction.

Came the second Tuesday of November 1932. The people who had so enthusiastically elected "the great engineer" in 1928 emphatically repudiated him at the polls. The man who talked of "a New Deal" was swept into power. When the day for his inauguration was at hand the banking structure of the nation collapsed. The savings of millions were lost in the debris. Spurred on by a new executive and an applauding people, Congress passed a whole ream of new regulations for business and industry. NRA, AAA, TVA, CWA, PWA gave the alphabet a new significance for Americans. The coffers of the federal government were opened to feed the hungry and minister to a prostrate agriculture.

Four years passed. The Democratic party, after decades of experience as a minority group, found itself more firmly entrenched in power than any party had been for half a century. When the election returns were in, even the staid and conservative Supreme Court astonished the country by a complete reversal of its attitudes on governmental regulation of economic affairs.

Other things were happening. The United States —famous for being the great open-shop country of the world—witnessed a great stirring among its laboring classes. Unions were formed where they had been undreamed of before. Under the leadership of John L. Lewis the workers of the great mass-production industries—automobiles, steel, rubber, textiles—began to organize. The "sit down" strike was imported from France.

Detroit, automobile capital of the world, became the scene of a great struggle on the part of labor for the right to bargain collectively. Two of the

4

three big automobile makers recognized the unions. Big Steel gave in without a struggle. Unionism grew apace.

In the midst of the turmoil the wheels of industry started again. Factory production schedules crept upward toward the marks of 1929 and then surpassed them. Prosperity seemed about at hand. Yet lurking in the background were the millions still dependent upon their government for bread. In the closing months of 1937 business declined again. For a second time in a decade the economic machine stalled.

Not only America, but the whole world is in the grip of a great flux. Human affairs are changing. Civil wars, riots, bloodshed, war, and preparation for war bear witness.

Men react to the situation in many ways. Some long for the peace of their yesterdays. Millions drift —content to snatch the pleasures the present gives —unmindful of the past and heedless of the future. Some believe they are witnessing the birth pangs of a new and better order of human affairs. Others see only a swiftly approaching chaos. Multitudes are confused.

Past historians have been much concerned with the doings of politicians and potentates, whom they regarded as the determiners of human destiny. Modern historians have come to see that kings and governments are more symptoms and results than causes. Political rulers are pawns moved about by larger and more significant forces. Those who would have insight into human affairs must probe beneath the froth of politics and examine the realities of common life. The way men make their living is the most important single fact about the character of a civilization.

But all too few recognize that back of the present political changes and the unrest which stirs the world lies one great cause. For nearly two centuries men have been changing their method of wresting food, shelter, and clothing from the earth. We are in the grip of a revolution—not basically political, but industrial. There is a new factor in the human equation. That factor is *machine production*. This revolution was started by the enterprising English in the eighteenth century and has gone forward at an accelerating pace. And the end is not yet. James Hargreaves, Richard Arkwright, and James Watt —a weaver, a barber, and an engineer—set it in motion.

The weaver was evidently lazy, for he was forever trying to discover means of getting out of work. He spun and wove enough to make a living but devoted much of his time to figuring out ways of making one motion do the work of two. The first result of his endless tinkering was a system of pulleys by which he could join two carding combs and exactly halve the time necessary for carding a fleece of wool. The efficiency of this simple device gave him added time for inventing. In 1762 he built a carding engine for a calico printer named Robert Peel. Peel saw possibilities in Hargreaves. He subsidized him as he devised things to make work easier.

Eventually he perfected a "Spinning Jenny"—named after Hargreaves' wife—which multiplied by eight the amount of thread which could be turned out by a single spinner. Fellow-workers regarded this new creation as "unfair competition." They broke into the inventor's home and smashed the machine. But they failed to destroy the idea. Hargreaves moved to a more tolerant community and proceeded to create a whole new set of problems for hand spinners by building a spinning mill, in 1768 at Nottingham.

Ten years later he died, little realizing that he had started a profound change in human affairs which historians would some day call "The Industrial Revolution."

Richard Arkwright was first a barber. Then he amassed a modest fortune as a mixer and merchant of hair dye. He has gone down in history as a great inventor. In 1767 he set to work to perfect cotton spinning machinery. He created the spinning mule. In 1771 he built a large factory at Cromford, in Derbyshire. The machinery in it was ingeniously devised and arranged with an eye to convenience and efficiency. He divided the labor among his employees so as to secure maximum production per man. He was the father of the factory system with its specialization and minute division of labor.

Arkwright's mill was run by water power. It remained for the third of the trio to give the factory system flexibility. He divorced it from its dependence upon falling water as a source of power.

The story of James Watt's perfecting of the steam engine is familiar to every school boy. A contemporary of Hargreaves and Arkwright, his work fitted beautifully with theirs to complete the pattern of industrial change. In 1790 a Watt engine was set to work driving the machinery of an Arkwright factory. Thus the machine age was born.

The succeeding years have witnessed the progressive application of machinery, power, and the factory system to the production of goods. The machine has replaced human hands; the steam engine and electric motor, the energy of the human body. Men once *made* goods with the use of simple tools; they now *tend* the machines which do the work. This development has progressively enveloped the industrial world. Even agriculture, last of the great industries to be affected, is today a changed occupation. The hoe, the sickle, the flail are all but forgotten instruments. The gang plow, the four-row cultivator, the combine, and the tractor have relegated them to the museums. Tending machines is occupying an increasing portion of the farmer's time.

The change to machine production upset a thousand equations: cut the race loose from moorings ancient as history. Previous to the work of Hargreaves, Arkwright, and Watt, industry was largely carried on in the home. The muscles of men or animals presented the chief source of productive power. Tools there were, but they simply increased the productive efficiency of muscular energy. Changes in the social structure—from slavery to feudalism to free labor—did nothing to disturb man's basic dependence on his own physical strength. They were simply varying means of controlling human labor and distributing the results of it. The advent of the machine did disturb this dependence.

Hargreaves' spinning jenny was hand driven, but when Arkwright used water power to turn the spindles and Watt made possible the use of steam power there was something different under the sun. New and untiring giants were put to work doing what man had always done with his own strength. Man was pygmied by these Goliaths. Human hands could not compete with them. Industry moved from home to factory. The ownership of machines became the fulcrum by which a new class raised itself to economic and political power. Those who could not own were given a single choice—tend machines or starve. The stomach is a tremendous factor in human affairs: they chose to tend machines.

9

For one hundred and fifty years mankind has been trying to adjust itself to this profound change in its sources and uses of energy. These years have inevitably been characterized by heaving turmoil.

This turmoil was started by the workers who saw in the machine a threat against their independence and security. The rioting spinners who destroyed Hargreaves' first machines were reacting blindly to the danger they did not fully understand. If they could have foreseen the events of succeeding decades they might have been more violent in their reaction. The replacement of men by machines has put on the backs of common folk a constant burden of making occupational changes. Whole trades, such as that of glass blower and carriage maker, have been wiped out, and those trained in them forced to find other means of earning their living. Over every occupation hangs the constant threat that the inventor's genius may make today's job unnecessary tomorrow. A new process or product may make the very thing produced obsolete and inefficient. So long as this is true there can be no security for those who have only the labor of their hands to exchange for bread.

Strikes, bread riots, hunger marches, trade unions, farm holidays, labor political parties are but expressions of the demand of those who cannot own machines for a measure of security. Violent protests will continue, and probably increase in virulence, until human society has learned to use machines in a manner which will bring respite from present strains and burdens.

It is doubtful indeed if the three men who started us into the machine age dreamed of the vast changes which were about to be ushered into the world. They seem to have been interested only in immediate and contemporary problems. Perhaps they had visions of great abundance for the human race and a new freedom from the scarcity which dependence on human energy had made inescapable.

But the machine age arrived with the triumph of the idea of individualism. The Middle Ages are often called the "dark ages." Unquestionably life did move at a leisurely pace and much of it was drab and dreary. However, it was characterized by a certain sense of social solidarity which made life bearable. The division of land and labor on the medieval manor did give a rough equality of access to the store of material wealth—meager as it was. There was a rather complete sharing of whatever of abundance or scarcity fell to the lot of the community. Within the cities the guilds fostered a sense of interdependence. Guild law required that men look after one another. Guild regulation saw to it that no man grabbed too big a share of wealth for himself.

The decay of feudalism brought all these things to an end. Men became individualists in their religion and in their business. Regulation of economic practices came to be regarded as old fashioned and outmoded.

It was just at the dawn of the machine age that Adam Smith published his *Wealth of the Nations*— bible of the cult which says that every businessman should do that which is right in his own eyes. It was his contention that business and industry should be wholly without governmental regulation. He was no believer in the benevolence of the trading class. He was committed to the idea that every man was out to make all he could for himself. Service to society was rendered solely for the purpose of accumulating private profits. But he felt that the best way to prevent exploitation of the public by these classes was to have free and unfettered competition. He believed that government regulation usually served the private interest of special groups much better than it did the public good. He suspected the motives of politicians as much as he did those of industrialists and traders. The eighteenth century witnessed the triumph of his ideas. A large portion of the time of the English parliament during the years from 1760 to 1800 was spent in repealing medieval laws regulating commerce and industry. Every man was left to do that which was to his greatest personal advantage in the very hour when machinery presented humanity with a new set of problems which needed the attention of the best collective intelligence of the race. The development

machine production was left entirely in the hands
those who saw in this new technique only a method
massing great wealth for themselves. The result
been untold suffering on the part of those whose
erty has forced them to sell the skill of their
ds for whatever machine owners were willing to

Despite the fact that the growth of this new tech-
e of production has been accompanied by much
less human misery, few intelligent people want
o back to the former dependence on hand labor.
hatma Gandhi of India has gained some pub-
y by talking of a return to the conditions of the
machine age. But his philosophy has no appeal
the American mind.

The average American is very much in love with
mechanical gadgets of our industrial civilization.
growth of invention has been intimately linked
our national history. We make heroes of our
ntists and inventors. Nations have worshiped
se who served them worse.

We love machines for what they will do for us
r the comforts they produce, for the drudgery
ch they save, for their efficiency in producing the
essities which sustain life and the luxuries which
ch it. They have made our thunderous cities pos-
e and freed us from a thousand natural terrors.
n 19. 6 when a great drouth destroyed the entire
est f many parts of our nation, famine did not

13

follow. Food poured into the stricken areas ov
transportation system dependent on a thousan
tricate mechanisms for its proper functioning.
centuries before would have seen death and sta
tion sweeping across the land.

When the Ohio valley was swept by a delug
1937 there was a remarkably low loss of life. C
alties were counted in tens, not thousands. The p
lation moved out ahead of the water by motor l
truck, train, and airplane. Radios hurled warn
through the ether and co-ordinated the work of
rescue parties. Without these, whole cities w
probably have seen the mud left in streets
houses made ghastly fertile with the bodies of
citizens. It did not happen because of mach
Flood and famine are great terrors only in t
countries which have despised or never heard of
inventor's genius.

We will not repudiate the machines. They ar
too useful. We love to be served by them. Like
entire human race, we are inherently lazy. We
only because we must. History proves how little
really care for labor. No leisure class has ever v
tarily given up its right to loaf. Every leisure c
when threatened, has defended with violence
privilege of living without working. However
lip service is paid to the virtue of industry, t
who have been able to escape labor by own ng sl
or serfs or clipping coupons have regar ed

work as a habit not intended for personal practice. In spite of all the problems that they have brought we will not cease loving to have our work done by giants of steel. Why should we?

One hundred and fifty years of industrialism is not to be repudiated. But an ever increasing number demand respite from the insecurity which is a part of life today. Natural disasters such as drouth, unprecedented cold, floods have lost many of their terrors, but haunting fears of loss of employment, of facing old age without resources, of loss of home or land have taken their place.

In an effort to rid themselves of these new enemies of human well-being, the race is experimenting with new forms of social and political organization. Three of these—Fascism, Socialism, and Communism—enjoy the greatest publicity.

Fascism is an effort to freeze civilization into stability by force. It attempts to preserve *as is* the inequalities and injustices of the present situation. It turns the direction of national affairs over to a small clique headed by a dictator. That clique tells others what they can and cannot do. It does away with political parties; it stops industrial strife by forbidding strikes; it stops discussion of economic and social problems by curtailing freedom of the press, free speech, and free assembly. It distracts the attention of the masses from their bread-and-butter problems by dragging out the brass bands, the flags, by creating parades, by patriotic and nationalistic oratory. Those who refuse to be distracted are clubbed into silence.

Countries under Fascism have a peace of a kind. In part it is peace born of fear to voice any but the *approved* opinion. It is in part the peace that comes from an intense sense of belonging to and serving with fanatical devotion something bigger than one's self. Its setting up of the state as a god to be served with complete and self-effacing devotion has brought some of the comfort that dogmatic religion always gives. But Fascism utterly fails to harness machines to the task of enriching human life. It cannot permanently work because it leaves untouched the basic causes of our present unrest. It may succeed in temporarily hypnotizing the people of a distraught country but it leaves their basic problems unsolved. Its constant appeal to national grandeur and to military adventure is a terrible sowing of the dragon's teeth.

Communism and Socialism call for a drastic reorganization of society—particularly of its property relationships. They would substitute collective ownership for private ownership and use the government as a means of making the change. They alike call on the disinherited workers to organize themselves for ownership of our industrial machinery. When the people own them, machines will be put to work serving all.

16

They differ seriously in the methods by which they propose to reach this end. Communism, like Fascism, relies strongly on dictatorship and violence.

The Communists say the successful winning of a violent class war is the first step toward bringing peace and security to mankind. They ask the disinherited to unite in a single great army, capable of seizing power in a revolution. They point to Russia as the great example of the successful use of their method. No one can deny that the Communists did wage successful war against the rulers of Tsarist Russia. They did it because they won the sympathy of that nation's armed forces. They capitalized the Russian soldier's thorough disgust with the World War. He had had his fill of death and mud and cooties and was glad enough to take it out on those who had forced such things on him. Even Trotsky admits that conditions were just right for the successful use of the Communistic method. He further admits that their success was largely dependent on the insight of Lenin who guessed right as to when violence would work. Had he guessed wrong, it might have been another story.

The Communists invite to a great gamble. On the surface their program has a direct and ruthless simplicity. They decree death to the owning class. Death has a complete and inescapable finality. Yet when all the complications are considered—the necessity of controlling armed forces, of guessing the right

17

moment for direct action, of waiting for the day when conditions are properly ripe for success—the semblance of simplicity disappears. The Communists boast of the certainty of their method. Its very uncertainty is its chief practical weakness.

Communism will appeal to the irresponsible and the desperate. Those who have lost their last piece of land or their last opportunity for securing subsistence wages may embrace it. The rest will have little stomach for risking their small stake in the present for the uncertainties of civil war.

Socialism repudiates Communism's trust in violence—except, perhaps, as a last resort, in case force is used in an attempt to defeat its program. The Socialist believes in democratic processes. He seeks to create the will to own in the disinherited, and to organize that will behind a vigorous and vigilant political party. When that party wins control of the forces of government then it will take over for the people the basic industries of the country. It will make these the property of the political state which will operate them for the good of all.

The proposal is simple enough, but those who advocate it have one serious blind spot for a fact of human history: politicians are inevitably controlled by property. Without regard for political belief or creed, political rulers are subservient to those who own the wealth of a nation. Political power is the result of economic power. The winning of an election is an empty victory for those who have no possessions. The Socialists have won elections and become heads of governments—in Germany, in England, in certain cities in the United States—but there has followed no sweeping reorganization of property relationships. The people have not become the owners of the industries of those nations or those cities. The government did not take control and administer the basic industries for the good of all. It attempted minor reforms and the correction of certain abuses, but little more.

There is little evidence that any large group of American people are interested in any of these three programs. Certainly neither the Communist nor the Socialist groups have had any remarkable growth during the great depression. The average American has an ingrained distrust of politicians which makes him shy at the idea of the government owning and controlling any large portion of industry. There is within his breast a love of doing and saying what he pleases, which creates considerable immunity to Fascism and Communism. Jittery people see tendencies in both directions and constantly raise the cry of "Wolf! Wolf!" but an increasing number respond to these alarms with a yawn.

If there is any one thing to which the American people are turning as a means of solving the problems which industrialism has created, it is to "collective bargaining." The rapid growth of labor unions, first under the spur of the collective bargaining clause of the National Recovery Act and more recently under the generalship of John L. Lewis and his Committee for Industrial Organization, bears its own evidence to this fact.

The great mass production industries—automobiles, steel, rubber—have each in turn been assaulted by the wave of unionization. Back of the movement lies the idea that since capital is organized to bargain collectively, labor must be also. By demanding shorter hours and better wages and by securing the right to bargain for these things as a group, labor has hopes of eliminating many of the uncertainties and insecurities now oppressing it. Many of the more enlightened industrial magnates have, with some reluctance, come to accept unionization as a necessary part of a changing world. Our liberal newspapers and journals have proclaimed this wave of interest in labor organization as a great turning point in our social and industrial life. Congress, through the Wagner Labor Relations Act, has said that men have a right, when they so desire, to be unhampered in their purpose to sell the labor of their hands collectively. The Supreme Court has declared that the founding fathers of our federal constitution did not deny men this privilege. Many Socialists, losing faith in the political future of their party, have turned to this newly-born labor movement as the great hope for the common man's tomorrow.

However, this emphasis on labor organization may be regarded by our future historians as just another evidence of our failure to realize that an industrial revolution has taken place which is to an increasing degree replacing hand labor with mechanical tools of production. The organization of labor is the organization of a force which is destined to have less and less significance in human affairs. The industrial revolution first rendered useless the hand tools of laborers. Today the need for hands gradually disappears.

Our inventors are still busy making machinery more automatic. The attainment of 1929 production schedules in 1937 without the absorption of many millions of the unemployed is but an indication of industry's lessening need for human beings in its productive processes.

Our infatuation with labor organization is not the only evidence of our refusal to recognize that we are living in an age of machines. The dealings of the government with the unemployed reflect a like blindness to economic facts. It has created agencies such as the CWA and the WPA to give work to those without it. But in so doing it has regarded the machine as a plague. It has not placed men at work with the most efficient tools the age affords for the purpose of making them as useful as possible in creating new goods for human consumption and enjoyment. Rather it has kept men busy with the aged pick and shovel. It encouraged inefficiency just because public opinion somehow wants to associate the putting in of hours of drudgery with the right to consume goods. That association is a hang-over from the days when the inefficiency of hand production made back-breaking toil necessary for human survival.

The tendency of many to regard unemployment as the basic problem of our age is another case in point. Men refuse to recognize the fact that the race has gone so far in solving its production problems that the necessity for human drudgery is vanishing with the hoe and sickle. There will be increasing *unemployment* at productive tasks in the future. Only a death sentence for every inventor of labor-saving machinery can prevent that. There will be less work to do. What we have to decide is whether or not the work that does need doing shall be distributed among all the able bodied of the nation with adequate distribution of consumers' goods to all. We can, of course, continue the present situation in which many at both ends of the social scale live in idleness while those who are so unfortunate as to be poor, as well as idle, eke out an existence on some sort of dole. The problem of *unemployment,* as we know it now, will disappear when men tackle the problem of proper distribution of consumers' goods.

The labor problem is not the fundamental issue. The right to bargain collectively for wages and hours does not touch the basic need for abundant consumption. The careful studies of the conservative Brookings Institute should prove to every skeptic that if America were exploiting her own capacity to produce, poverty could be ended. America is not exploiting her capacity to produce because the present system of distribution has bottle-necked the process. There will come release for the masses from insecurity and uncertainty only when we cease being engrossed with the problems of the producer alone and give time and attention to the interests of the consumer.

Collective bargaining for higher wages and shorter hours appears to be a way of increasing consumption. It does enable those who work to get better wages, but so long as the owners of industry can pass on higher labor costs to the consumer in higher prices nothing has happened. The workers may handle more money in the course of a year but more money in itself does not mean greater purchasing power. It does not mean enlarged access to the great reservoirs of goods which we can turn out with our present productive facilities.

There must be something more than unionization of labor. Working for that alone is as futile as fussing around with the pumps and storage tanks of a city water system whose mains, lead-in lines, and house plumbing have failed. If we solve the pressing problems of our age it will be because we become

23

concerned with the building of a new system of distribution.

Those whom the machine age has disinherited must acquire the ownership of the stores, the wholesales, and the productive machinery which makes and distributes goods. There must be organization of the consumers toward that end.

Fortunately we do not have to forge the techniques for giving such ownership to the people today. Others who have gone before us have shown the way. Over a century ago some of those whom the industrial revolution had deprived of ownership of the tools of production began experimentation with consumer ownership. Out of their trials and errors, and eventually their successes, was born the Consumers Co-operative movement—a method by which millions the world round are becoming owners both of machines and the channels of distribution through which goods are placed in their hands. However, they are not achieving ownership as workers, as producers. They are achieving it as consumers. There is a difference.

For an understanding of this movement and its technique of organizing business we must retrace some history. We must first visit nineteenth-century England.

CHAPTER II

A Prophet In the Land

THE FIRST REACTIONS to the Industrial Revolution were almost wholly instinctive and unreasoned. Workers saw in the factories only a threat against their livelihood. Some organized themselves into machine destroying mobs. Industrialists saw a golden chance to make profits. The world was hungry for goods. Machines offered a chance to satisfy that hunger—for a price. The lust for wealth drove those who could afford it to build factories, and hire, for as little as possible, the laborers whose hand-production was rendered obsolete.

This meant misery and squalor. The slums arrived with the factory. England became a land of deserted villages—vividly described by Goldsmith—and factory towns, where poverty stalked the streets. Before many years had passed owners made a discovery: the nimble fingers of little children could tend whirling spindles and power looms. Child labor began. Men and women lived in idleness, supported by their little ones. Or else the whole family was put to work to secure a pittance that kept body and soul together on a plane that could not be called a healthy animal existence. Human flesh was cheap.

The owners of industry did not care. They were interested in the golden stream that flowed into their coffers. Riches and misery grew side by side—parts of the same sordid story.

But every action brings its reaction. In the mind of a man named Robert Owen came the first prophetic revulsion against this heartless exploitation. He realized that humanity had a new factor with which to deal; he foresaw the tremendous changes which new methods of production would bring in human affairs. He believed that those changes could be intelligently guided into constructive channels. He felt that the new misery and the new wealth were not necessarily bound together. Only blindness and irresponsibility kept them so. He saw in the machine a productive instrument capable of blessing all whom it affected. He had faith that the factory system could be reformed, and a quality rare in men—willingness to have reform begin with himself.

Owen was an owner of machines and a good businessman—in the usual meaning of the term. At eighteen he controlled a half interest in a factory employing forty workers. He made his start on five hundred dollars of borrowed money, and sold out at the end of one year at a substantial profit. At nineteen he was a factory manager in Manchester. So well did he handle the force of five hundred people who worked under him that he was given a partnership in the business. Shortly thereafter he sold out again and became manager and partner in the New Lanark Mills.

Here between two and three thousand men, women, and children lived and worked under typical conditions of poverty and filth. The hours of labor for all hands were from six in the morning until seven at night. Parents brought their children to work after their seventh year. Nearly five hundred orphans from nearby work-houses were there under the despotic rule of factory management. Owen's biographer describes conditions thus: "Deep poverty drove the workers to the mills from the cities; and the work-house authorities gladly—to get rid of them—sent a cartload of orphans, aged six and seven, now and again. The general character may be deduced. Their homes were foul. Their habits primitive. Their streets were sewers. The public houses were infamous. Thieving, lying, swearing, drinking, and fighting were as common as the squalor with which they spattered the golden valley"—of the Clyde.

Owen spent fifteen years remaking New Lanark. In 1800 he quietly resolved that poverty, destitution, and ignorance would not be by-products of the excellent cotton goods he was producing. He did everything that a benevolent capitalist could do: cut the hours of labor, put the children in school at the expense of the mills, paid wages that made decent living possible, cleaned up the streets, established company stores that sold excellent goods at reasonable prices. New Lanark became a model factory town, known all over Europe for being the one bright spot in terrible industrial dreariness. The workers responded to kindness and justice. They changed with their environment.

But Owen had partners to deal with. They tolerated his fantastic ideas only because he produced fat dividends even while spending money on these unheard-of efforts to transform factory working conditions. Eventually, however, their love of profits caused them to interfere. They reasoned that returns might have been even greater had there been none of this social experimentation. By 1809 the first set of associates had become disgusted and sold out—at a handsome profit. In 1811 the second group complained like the first and only with the help of rich and public-spirited Quakers was Owen able to keep control of his beloved community. With some help and some hindrance from them he continued with his experiment until 1816. By that time the results were so unmistakable that he believed the hour was at hand to publicize them before the world.

He felt that he had found a way by which society could be transformed. His formula included universal education, elimination of child labor, reduction of working hours for adults to ten per day, the institution of public works to absorb those who could

not find employment in private industry, the abolition of religious intolerance and war, drastic revision
of the criminal code, and basic reformation of jails
and the administration of justice—a program not
dissimilar to parts of our New Deal.

He made his first appeal to his own class—the
factory owners. He simply asked that they do what
his success at New Lanark proved could be done.
Later he asked his government to sponsor his program. The owners of industry saw in his schemes
only a serious interference with profits. Officehold-
ers were more inclined to give the matter serious
consideration, but in the face of the hostility of the
industrialists, they would do nothing. Owen's appeal
fell on deaf ears. The real and nominal rulers of
a great nation were little interested in lessening the
blow which the invention of machinery had struck
against the peace and security of common folk. They
were interested only in profits and in their own political careers.

Then came the end of the Napoleonic wars. Peace
came to Europe after long and bitter struggles
against the France of the first Napoleon. Peace
brought its turmoil. The usual post-war business
reaction set in. Unemployment stalked the land.
Wages were forced down. Misery increased. Owen
saw that war and killing had increased business
profits, brought a kind of feverish prosperity, while
peace brought poverty and deprivation for thou-

sands upon thousands. He pondered the fact and began to wonder if a business system that thrived in war and languished in peace could be anything but rotten at its core.

The increased suffering of the masses resulted in strikes, hunger marches, and riots. The government which had refused to consider Owen's reform program was willing to resort to ruthless violence to quell the rioting of hungry men—and did.

Owen watched the events of these troubled years with growing disillusionment. He lost all hope of getting favorable consideration of his plans from those in high places. Love of money rather than love of men was too deeply rooted in the hearts of factory owners for them to take Owen's appeal seriously. He saw that changes would have to come by other methods than those he first considered workable. The importance of restoring ownership to those who had lost their property slowly dawned on him. He gradually came to think in terms of what factory workers could do for themselves rather than what he could get others to do for them.

He clearly saw that individualistic ownership of the tools of production was out of the question, so far as the laborers were concerned, under the factory system. Collective ownership alone seemed possible. With heroic abandonment he set himself to the task of making the workers owners of their factories. He financed workers' colonies in which there

was social ownership of land and factories. In these
colonies he established democratic control and constantly emphasized the ideal of working together for
common good. But his "Villages of Co-operation
and Union" failed. Owen had too great faith in the
inherent goodness of human nature. He did not
realize how completely the dominant spirit of individualism had rendered men incapable of intelligent social action. Medieval habits of communal living had been too long forgotten to be easily revived.
Then, too, the problems of factory production, labor management, and profitable sale of things produced were too complex for the workers to handle.
They were utterly without administrative experience
and without a schoolmaster to train them.

One of those colonies was established on American soil. New Harmony, Indiana, was Owen's New
World experiment. It went the same route taken by
the Old World efforts. Failure was the common end.
All these attempts served only to demonstrate that
ownership could not be *given* to the people. They
must claim it for themselves.

While the colonies were failing, the disinherited
workers were beginning to do things for themselves.
Trade Unionism slowly got under way against the
combined hostility of industry and government.
Owen gave his blessing to the movement. He helped
form the Grand National Trades Union of Great
Britain and Ireland—a federation of labor unions.

Within six months the organization was suppressed. But it was a beginning. The victims of machine production had begun to demand a voice in their own destiny.

Until his death in 1858 this man gave every encouragement to the workers to organize themselves: into trade unions for securing better wages and working conditions; into little productive societies in which there was common ownership of a small factory or workshop. Following a builders' strike in Birmingham in 1833 he even recommended that they organize their own stores so that they could have control over sources of food and household necessities. He saw that the organized strength of the weak might, if rightly directed, become a sure defense against the heartlessness of the mighty.

Owen died a poor man. He had spent a fortune in an effort to solve a problem which was too big for him. Years of talking, writing, and lavish expenditure of funds yielded but very meager results. His dreams were unfulfilled. Judged by ordinary standards he died a failure.

He takes no place in history for his practical accomplishments. He is honored because he was the first to attempt to deal intelligently with the problems which the coming of machine production has created for the human race. He made the mistakes any beginner would have made. It is not surprising that he failed to do anything more than focus attention on the major issues. We are deeply indebted to him for starting men in search of a solution. He did demonstrate that squalor and human wretchedness were not necessarily a part of the industrial picture.

The evolution of his thinking is interesting for us. He first tried to change the world by example. New Lanark was his great illustration of what could be done in an industrial hell. He found that most men were not even interested in what he had accomplished. He started out with a simple faith in the goodness of governments and in the possibilities of the political method of solving social problems. He discovered that the welfare of men without property is not a very serious concern of the state. He came to see that only those who are adversely affected by bad conditions will give sustained support to a program of changing them. He sensed the importance of property ownership in the affairs of men and advocated that those who are too poor to own property individually pool their resources and own together. His final belief was that when men discovered how to own together they would have in their hands the key to their own destiny.

Owen did not show how it could be done. It remained for others, more lowly in wealth and culture than he, to perfect a method by which men of poverty could quietly and yet successfully make themselves men of property.

33

CHAPTER III

Revolution In a Grocery Store

THE FOURTH DECADE of the past century has been nick-named "the hungry forties." The western world was enjoying one of the periodic business depressions which have been an ever recurring affliction during one hundred and fifty years of expanding industrialism. Political upheavals, bread riots, strikes, unemployment, suffering, were all a part of the history of that time. Factory workers and small farmers were facing difficult problems. For upon them, as usual, fell the heaviest burdens of want and privation. There was no government relief or unemployment insurance to dull the edge of their suffering. Many had no work; those who did found wages cut to the bone. They were troubled years.

One of the groups particularly hard hit were the flannel weavers of a city of north England, called Rochdale. Desperation drove them to a strike in 1843. The strikers faced all the difficulties involved in trying to get higher wages in a day when the labor market is glutted with those who have no work. It was inevitable that the strike fail. Nor were the factory owners slow to take advantage of its collapse. When others went back to work those who led

the walkout found that their services were no longer
desired. All the factories of the city boycotted them;
a black list of such trouble makers had been prepared
and circulated effectively.

The loss of that strike was to them tragedy indeed. It meant the eclipse of their hope for better
living conditions. It meant the deepening of a misery
that was already more than they felt able to bear.
But out of their loss was born the technique that
Robert Owen had failed to discover. The black-listed
strike leaders of Rochdale found a way by which
they could make themselves men of property.

It was in part the result of seeds Owen had
planted. Some of these men had heard of his idea
of workers owning property together. They had
dreamed dreams of worker-ownership of mills and
factories. Even before the strike they had experi-
mented and failed in attempting to own their own
stores.

Talk was one thing these men could afford. They
spent long hours discussing their problems and won-
dering what they could do by way of self-deliverance.
It was one way of making their lot more bearable.
Eventually from their conversation grew a conviction: the way out was to go into business for themselves.

Out of that conviction grew an organization.
They called it the "Equitable Society of Rochdale
Pioneers." Their basic purpose was to make them-

selves their own employers. With pathetic courage they stated the ambitious objectives of their association in the following language:

"The establishment of a store for the sale of provisions, clothing, etc.

"The building, purchasing, or erecting of a number of houses in which those members, desiring to assist each other in improving their domestic and social conditions, may reside.

"The manufacture of such articles as the society may determine upon, to provide employment of such members who may be without employment, or who may be suffering in consequence of repeated reduction in their wages.

"The purchasing, or renting of an estate or estates of land, which shall be cultivated by members who may be out of employment, or whose labor is badly remunerated.

"And further: that as soon as practicable this society shall proceed to arrange powers of production, distribution, education, and government—or, in other words, to establish a self-supporting home colony of united interests, or assist other societies in establishing such colonies."

Whatever they may have lacked in resources, the Rochdale Pioneers certainly had no lack of ambition. They were boldly proclaiming their intention of solving problems that had given pause to Robert Owen with all his wealth, and which had baffled the statesmen of Europe. They were out to take possession of the earth: to become owners of stores, manufacturing enterprises, land, educational institutions, and government. They would become men of property.

In the beginning there were twenty-eight members of this seemingly mad society—about to do battle with the giants of a lusty young industrial capitalism. One woman was among the company. Her name was Ann Tweedale.

The Pioneers started their ambitious schemes in a most unspectacular manner. They began by saving money. It was a slow, painful process for there was little money on which they could lay their hands. It was about all they could do to keep body and soul together. But they got a halfpenny here and a twopence there. Halfpennies and twopences will eventually add up into shillings, and shillings into pounds. At the end of a year they had twenty-eight English pounds: $140 in American money. It wasn't much, but they believed it to be enough to take the first step in their plan.

A store was opened in an old warehouse basement on Toad Lane on the night of December 21, 1844. Its meager stock could have been hauled home in one large wheelbarrow. It consisted of sugar, oatmeal, flour, butter, and candles. The total value was $70. When the shutters were taken down for the opening, rowdy street urchins shouted their derision. The "ow'd weavers' shop" wasn't much of a store. In the beginning it was open for business two nights a week and the clerking was done by unpaid volunteers.

It was many months before the business was large enough to justify its staying open for six days in the week with a full time manager in charge but eventually that day came. The store grew as if it had within itself something of the strange power of a fertilized cell to grow into an active self-directing organism. At the end of the first year the membership had grown to seventy-four; the capital to $900. The first annual report contained the cheerful news that $3,500 had trickled across the counter and a net saving of $160 achieved.

Robert Owen passed away in 1858, probably without ever having heard of the Rochdale society. But three years later its membership totaled two thousand families, and the capital $75,000. When the golden jubilee of the opening of the store was celebrated in 1894, membership was twelve thousand and the annual volume of business $1,500,000.

The Pioneers were not only great dreamers; they were also successful businessmen. Success did not come, however, without some difficulties. As early as 1850 a crisis developed which all but carried their venture down the road which Owen's co-operative villages had taken. Mild achievement brought ambitions for expansion, so at the turn of the half-century the society decided to buy a flour mill. It looked like a means of taking them one step further into the program they had cut out for themselves. However, they failed to take account of all the factors involved.

First, it is one thing to manufacture a product: it is another to market it. The mill made much more flour than the store needed to supply its customers and it wasn't an easy matter to dispose of the surplus. Private merchants weren't overly eager to buy from an organization maintaining a retail outlet in competition with them. Second, people do not always like what is good for them. The Pioneers resolved in the very beginning to handle only good quality products which were neither doctored nor adulterated. The flour which the mill produced was slightly yellow—as is all unbleached flour. But the housewives of Rochdale had bought flour bleached with alum for so long that they had little use for the yellowish stuff now offered them. Only time and education made a place for unbleached flour on the tables of Rochdale consumers.

For three years the mill produced excellent flour and husky financial losses—losses which frightened the faint-hearted and set the tongues of calamity prophets to wagging. Capital began to be withdrawn from the society; members threatened to withdraw. But, at last, with the help of other groups who were copying their methods a market for the surplus was found and the mill became a paying proposition.

Reserves, wisely set aside during the first years of operation of the store, were sufficient to absorb the losses on this first experiment in manufacturing. The storm blew over and was forgotten. Years brought increasing confidence in the whole enterprise. Faith, business volume, capital investment, and membership in the society grew together.

The organization of the Rochdale Pioneers was the beginning of Consumers Co-operation, a development which slowly envelops the world. The movement is active in practically every country on the globe. Wherever it is found it is creating a new class of property owners. Its membership today is not known exactly but it is pretty safe to say that not less than 65,000,000 families are identified with it.

The Rochdale society was not England's first co-operative. It was not even the first to attempt the operation of a store. Between the years 1828 and 1832 there arose in Great Britain what is known as the Union Shop movement. Its guiding spirit was a London physician named William King. Dr. King ministered to working-class families. He saw their suffering and their frequent illnesses—caused so largely by their poverty. He became deeply concerned about the conditions which the industrial revolution had created and, like Owen, wanted to do something about them. He was a disciple of the first great prophet of modern times but not subservient to his thinking. He attached greater importance to consumer action. Perhaps his experience as a physician made him much more conscious of the need for better food and clothing in poor families than was Owen, the successful *producer*. Perhaps he saw in the operation of something as simple as a store, a technique that was within the range of the ability of English laborers. Anyway, he did encourage the co-operative ownership of stores by consumers as a means by which the poor could do something toward helping themselves.

By 1830 there were one hundred and seventy Union Shops scattered over England. A Union Shop was a society of workers organized as consumers. By 1832 the number had grown to four hundred. Dr. King published a magazine called *The Co-operator* in which he encouraged these organizations and tried his best to guide them to success. Many thoughtful people felt that the Union Shops were destined to play an important role in the future of the nation's poorer people. But the next two years shattered their dreams. One by one the stores began to collapse. By 1835 only here and there among the Scotch and North Englanders were Union Shops to be found. The rest had failed. The few that did survive were forgotten and rediscovered by a later generation, made *store*-conscious by the Rochdale success.

There were several causes which contributed to the collapse of the Union Shops. Those causes can be summed up in a single word—inexperience. Store-keeping had for generations been wholly a matter of private enterprise. No one knew how to make it a social undertaking. King, and the other intellectuals who assisted in giving the movement leadership, were as completely in the dark about organizational techniques as those whom they attempted to help.

Some of the Union Shops failed because they did a credit business; some because they became involved in price wars with richer and wiser competitors. Not a few were destroyed by inner strife brought on by efforts to control the religion, morals, and politics of members. Some were robbed by directors and managers who stole their funds—taking advantage of the fact that these organizations had no legal standing and hence no protection under the law. Some were destroyed by their very prosperity. They made money but had no acceptable way of distributing the funds created. A part paid dividends on shares as did the ordinary business firm. The primary interest of shareholders came to center on dividends and all co-operative features were forgotten. Other groups used their profits to set up manufacturing enterprises in which members were given employment. In these, jealousy arose between those who were given work and those who wanted it. A number of the Union Shops had permitted men to vote according to the number of shares they held. If they were prosperous the larger shareholders eventually gained control and operated the business for their own personal advantage.

The Rochdale Pioneers succeeded because of their canny ability to profit by the mistakes of others. They knew the Union Shop movement and had the intelligence to learn from its failures.

They refused to be political, religious, or moral partisans. If they had insisted on allegiance to any political or religious creed as a qualification for membership they would have had the merriest kind of dog fight in the very beginning. Among the original twenty-eight were Owenites, Christian Socialists, Chartists, and even ardent temperance advocates. Toleration was essential to the very life of their organization. They practiced the principle of religious and political neutrality from the very beginning. It remained their practice through the passing years.

In order to avoid price wars they decided to charge the current market prices on the goods they sold. They avoided the pitfalls of a credit business by insisting on cash trading. In order that members might be kept accurately informed as to the affairs of the business they insisted on frequent and regular audits of the books.

Control was placed in the hands of a board of directors, democratically elected by the membership. Each member was allowed but one vote in all elections and only those who would take the trouble to attend meetings were allowed the franchise. Proxy voting was not permitted.

They believed that those who created the capital for the operation of their business should have some reward for so doing. That reward they set at five per cent interest, which was the current rate.

What to do with earnings above five per cent on capital was a tough problem. The mistakes of the Union Shops were very fresh in their memory. And yet to find a detour around them was not easy. There were no precedents to guide them. Something new was necessary. Originality is rare indeed. Long hours of discussion simply took them back over familiar paths. Finally one of their number had a happy thought: why not give back the earnings to the patrons of the business on the basis of their patronage? After all the patrons created the earnings. Each patron contributed to them in exact proportion to the amount he purchased through the society. The problem was solved. This simple scheme was adopted. It was freighted with great wisdom.

This method of distributing earnings was the one original thing in the Rochdale formula. Their other practices had precedents in the varied experiments of the Union Shop movement. It is extremely doubtful if any other method would have worked. It had the double virtue of being thoroughly just and of giving those who supported the store, a tangible in-hand reward for faithful support. The patronage refund is rooted in human realism. It appeals at once to man's sense of fairness and to his self-interest.

Also the Pioneers had the foresight to see that an intelligent membership is essential to the proper functioning of democratic group effort. Though most of them were illiterate, they had no boorish disrespect for knowledge. Rather they were determined to equip themselves intellectually for the role which they hoped to play in changing the status of the exploited laborer. Accordingly, they determined from the very beginning that their co-operative society should also be an educational institution. They used some of the earnings of the business for the maintenance of a library and a reading room. They constantly sought to make themselves and others intelligent about their business, general economics, and the social order in which they lived.

The Rochdale practices have long since been worked into a simple code of behavior for consumers' co-operative societies. The laws of this code are usually given as follows:

First, there are three rules called the *Fundamental Principles of Consumers' Co-operation.*

(1.) Democratic control. That means one vote per member without regard to the number of shares held. Owning one share or ten makes no difference in control. Members vote as persons, and not as owners of a given portion of the capital.

(2.) Returns to capital shall not be more than

45

the minimum prevailing rate of interest. Dividends do not go skyrocketing with earnings. The Pioneers set the interest rate at five per cent but the percentage is left to the discretion of the members of each society. This principle eliminates speculation. Co-operative shares do not fluctuate in value with earnings.

(3.) After operating expenses are paid, reserves and education cared for, interest paid, the remainder of earnings are distributed to patrons on the basis of patronage. The one who spends the most with a society gets the most in return.

With these principles go certain methods which are sometimes called the *Methods of Consumers' Co-operation;* sometimes the *Secondary Principles of Consumers' Co-operation.*

(1.) Open membership. No one shall be denied membership in a co-operative society unless it is known he wishes to join for the purpose of making trouble for the organization.

(2.) Political and religious neutrality. Members shall be left free to support any or no political or religious sect as conscience dictates.

(3.) Non-members may buy their way into membership. They may do it by purchasing a share of stock or by simply giving their trade to the organization. Non-members often receive their portion of the patrons' refund in terms of credit toward their initial shares. As soon as the refund equals the value of a share of stock the patron automatically becomes a member with full voting privileges.

(4.) A portion of the earnings shall be spent for the education of members and non-members. Usually, though not always, education is confined to spreading knowledge of the techniques, philosophy, and history of co-operation.

(5.) Labor shall be fairly treated. Every effort is put forth to make working conditions as ideal as circumstances will permit.

(6.) Business shall be done for cash.

(7.) Current market prices shall be charged.

(8.) Adequate reserves for depreciation, expansion, and unforeseen difficulties shall be regularly set aside.

(9.) Where possible, co-operative societies shall combine their strength in democratic associations for the purposes of wholesaling, manufacturing, and providing services too large to be undertaken by local organizations.

These things combined with intelligent management were responsible for the success of the Rochdale Pioneers. Experience has proven the soundness of their building. Where these principles have been violated failure has resulted. Where they have been adhered to, other groups have been able to achieve similar successes.

Between the years 1879 and 1889 eight hundred forty-four co-operative societies failed in England.

Those failures were largely the result of violation of some part of the above code. Similar failures elsewhere have largely been due to the same cause. In the hard school of experience men have learned the necessity of strict adherence to Rochdale practice. It is essential to success.

CHAPTER IV

Progress

NOTHING SUCCEEDS LIKE SUCCESS. As soon as the
Pioneers had demonstrated that co-operatively
owned stores were a practical possibility, the dis-
tressed workers of other communities began to organize societies. During 1847 and 1848 stores were
started in a number of nearby towns: Bacup, Tod-
morden, Leigh, Salford, Padiham, and Middletown.
These were all in north England not far from the
Scottish border. Perhaps it took the English ability
to muddle through, influenced by the thrift of the
Scotch, to make a success of the plodding idea that
organizing co-operative stores had something to do
with changing the status of those who earn their
bread by the sweat of their brow.

By 1852 there were one hundred and thirty societies in north England and the Scottish Midlands.
Some of these operated on the Rochdale plan; some
did not. Some were the isolated survivors of the
Union Shop debacle. They were all small. Their
average membership was fifty. Rochdale stood head
and shoulders above the rest with its six hundred.
By 1860 all were operating on the Rochdale plan.

Three years later the total number of societies was four hundred twenty-six.

The years since 1850 had witnessed a growing sense of common purpose among them. In '63 the first steps were taken toward setting up a commercial federation for furthering mutual ends. The Rochdale society took the lead in calling together representatives of the various local groups for the discussion of common problems. From that time onwards such conferences were a regular feature of the co-operative calendar. The sense of unity ripened into the conviction that co-operation between co-operatives might have in it greater possibilities than just the exchange of ideas. A buying federation was the logical next move.

The steps by which this idea took form cannot be accurately traced. As early as 1859 William Cooper of Rochdale suggested that the Pioneers might undertake to act as a wholesaling agent for some of the nearby smaller societies. A small group of experienced store founders considered the idea of a co-operative wholesale in 1860. That year witnessed the establishment of a little news sheet called *The Co-operator* which advocated the establishment of such a central organization.

At a meeting held on Good Friday in 1863 the representatives of some of the leading organizations committed themselves to the creation of "The North of England Co-operative Wholesale Agency and

Depot Society, Limited." By the close of the year the wholesale society—burdened with its sonorous name —had been organized. Business operation began in 1864.

Five years of thinking, planning, and hard work were behind the formation of the wholesale but its first years did not altogether justify the roseate dreams of its founders. It was the creation of men whose vision encompassed the coming years. Not all members of local societies were interested in the future. Most of them were much more concerned with the immediate task of keeping their retail enterprises on an even keel. Store managers, who had gotten used to bargaining with private wholesales and had developed pride in their ability to haggle in the general market, did not feel very great enthusiasm for giving the bulk of their trade to this new organization. The first report and balance sheet of the wholesale showed that only fifty-four societies had become shareholders in it and but thirty-two of those had bothered to send delegates to the semi-annual meeting.

But though the existing provincialism and backwardness of societies and managers slowed up growth, it did not check it. 1866 saw the turnover of the wholesale pass the million dollar mark. The success of that year's business was the turning point. The next year business jumped fifty per cent and saw two hundred and fifty societies in active support of it.

Then came home building. At a cost of $20,000 a six-story headquarters building was erected at the corner of Balloon Street and Garden in Manchester. Early in 1869 it was dedicated with fitting ceremonies.

It was a modest step forward in the quiet assumption of property ownership by people of small means —whose sole economic power lay in the shillings they traded across the counters of retail stores.

In 1868 the Scotch followed in the footsteps of their English cousins. They founded a wholesale society at Glasgow.

In the meantime the societies of northeast England were complaining about the distance from Manchester to the river Tyne. They wanted wholesaling service nearer home. They persuaded the wholesale's board of directors to establish a branch at Newcastle. They promised faithful and loyal support, and gave it. The branch opened with three employees in May, 1872. The first year's business topped $750,000. On January 2, 1874, a $65,000 home for the Newcastle offices and warehouses was opened.

By that year the number of co-operative stores in England had grown to nearly nine hundred. The aggregate membership was three hundred thousand families; the invested capital $15,000,000; the annual sales $50,000,000; net earnings $4,500,000. Scotland had two hundred stores, fifty thousand

members; sales totaled $7,500,000; net earnings
were $700,000; the capital invested $1,250,000.

Manufacturing was the next step. The first
products were biscuits and sweets. A factory was
purchased by the wholesale in 1873. Headaches for
the management and losses were the first results of
this venture. The machinery of the factory was anti-
quated and had to be modernized. Experienced
management was hard to find. It took three years
to get the venture on a paying basis but at last the
Crumpsall Biscuit works became a satisfactory part
of the co-operative empire. Boot and shoe manufacturing got under way in a rented factory the same
year the biscuit factory was purchased. This worked
out very well from the start. The plant was purchased in 1874 and enlarged a year later. A committee report given in December 1876 boasts of
producing 8,000 pairs of shoes a week with an em-
ployee group of over four hundred. Soap manufacturing started in 1874.

Thirty years after the opening of the Toad Lane
store at Rochdale saw the co-operators well launched
into the field of production. Another part of the
Pioneers' program had become a reality. It had not
come quite as they visualized it. Manufacturing had
not been undertaken primarily to provide employment for unemployed co-operators. The plants were
not owned by the Rochdale society alone. These
factories were started for the purpose of making

goods for consumers; they were owned by the co-operative wholesale society which was in turn owned by the eight hundred local co-operatives scattered across England. A third of a million families were represented in those local groups. The combined resources of those families did make it possible for them to join the ranks of owners of business and industry. They were building themselves an economic empire.

Another conquest came in 1876. The sea has a peculiar significance for the Britisher. Ruling the waves is an old custom with the people of Great Britain. Co-operators decided to share in that rule. They had reason to complain of the treatment given them by shipping companies so they bought the S.S. *Plover*, a little vessel of 250 tons. They found that ruling the waves secured for them many favors. The railroads lowered freight rates; continental merchants gave better prices. The *Plover* greeted a sister ship in 1879—the S.S. *Pioneer* of 650 tons. The *Cambrian* was added to the fleet in 1881.

The private shipping interests were greatly irritated by this invasion of their economic realm. A price war was declared. The co-operative wholesale decided to fight it out. A fourth ship was purchased. Shipping magnates openly expressed their contempt toward "working men butting in on something they knew nothing about." This but steeled the resolve of the co-operators to see the scrap through.

They cheerfully wrote off their losses until the "interests" sued for peace. An economic war had been waged and won. Vessel after vessel was added with the passing of time until a fleet of eleven ships carried goods for the co-operatives. Most of the boats were sold early in the present century because of changed conditions in the shipping trade. But the disinherited commoners had had a taste of ship-owning and they liked it.

It is interesting to note that in 1894, when Manchester was made a seaport by the completion of an expensive shipping canal to the ocean, the S.S. *Pioneer* was the first vessel to dock at the pier. The first cargo landed in Manchester, the seaport, was sugar from Rouen—imported for the tables of the *working class*. When the *Pioneer* was lashed to the dock, the Mayor of Salford was among those who stepped aboard to extend congratulations to the captain.

That incident is a symbol of the growing favor which co-operators enjoyed in the eyes of politicians. The Rochdale society had begun business in 1844 under the Friendly Societies Act of 1836. That act declared that such societies should do business only with members. The co-operators disregarded the provision. Their practice was made legal in 1852 by the passage of the Industrial and Provident Acts. In 1862 the bill was further amended at the request of co-operators in order to make legal the proposed

55

wholesale. Its amendment was materially aided by the reading of co-operative records in Parliament. The law makers were signally impressed with the cold facts and figures of business success. These acts were revised again in 1876 when the wholesale wanted to open a banking department. Those who own property are listened to in the halls of government.

Banking as a co-operative enterprise was first undertaken seriously in 1872. In that year a group of the northern societies organized an independent bank. Four years later it failed through mismanagement. Following the revision of co-operative law in the year of this failure the wholesale set up a banking department of its own. This second venture, begun with some misgivings, was successful from the very start. Co-operatives the country over used it as a depository for funds. Individual co-operators carried accounts with it. Credit was made available to societies needing it. The entire movement found the new bank a great source of economic strength.

Flour milling was one of the first manufacturing processes undertaken by co-operative societies. Attention has already been called to the first Rochdale venture in this field. Other societies likewise went into it. Some of the larger ones owned mills individually. In other cases federations of small groups were created and the mills were owned by the federations. By 1880 there were between thirty and forty of these small co-operatively owned mills. Until that time the wholesale, out of respect for local enterprises, had kept out of the milling field. But gradually it became apparent that flour milling was becoming a big business. Profit-making corporations were erecting plants capable of turning out hundreds of sacks a day. The small mills were not able to compete with these industrial Goliaths. Only one co-operative organization was big enough to undertake milling on the scale which the new conditions demanded. That was the wholesale. In 1886 the representatives of local societies, assembled in annual meeting, passed a resolution empowering the directors to build a plant.

They moved slowly at first, realizing the importance of a good location with needed rail and water transportation. They finally chose a site near Dunston on the Tyne. It was purchased and work started preparing the ground for the erection of the mill. In 1889 the need for it became suddenly urgent. Private manufacturers had set afoot plans for the creation of a national flour trust which would include all the large mills from Humber to the Tweed. The co-operators did not propose to be at the tender mercies of any such combination. They pushed their own project with renewed energy and at a cost of $600,000 built a plant having a capacity of forty sacks per hour. It was formally opened April 18, 1891, with great jubilation.

In spite of its elaborate birthday party it proceeded forthwith to lose money for its owners. At the end of four years the losses totaled $150,000. This was not altogether the fault of the management. The wheat market of the world had gone chaotic and there was no controlling it. When the market finally settled down the mill began to make money and continued to do so for long years.

Large as was the Dunston mill it was all too small to meet the co-operative market for flour. The wholesale continued to import great quantities of this household necessity. A second and larger plant was ready for work in 1900. No celebration was held when its wheels started turning. The deficits piled up by the first venture were too fresh in the memory. The third and fourth mills came in 1902 and 1910. When the wholesale—whose name had in the meantime been shortened to Co-operative Wholesale Society and popularly abbreviated to C.W.S.—celebrated its Golden Jubilee in 1913, the mills which it owned were turning out two hundred fifty sacks of flour each hour of the day and night.

Through the succeeding years the C.W.S. has steadily expanded. It is today the largest single food distributing business in the world. Its flour mills are the largest and most modern in the Empire; its textile factories hold a like position. It owns nearly one hundred and fifty manufacturing enterprises. These turn out not only food and clothing but automobiles and radios as well. Its properties include 30,000 acres of tea plantations in India and Ceylon, olive farms in Africa, acres and acres of farm land in England, producing food and drink for the 8,000,000 families which are now a part of the English consumers' co-operative movement. The banking department is fourth in financial strength to the Bank of England. The general insurance department, established in 1898, is writing one-half the insurance of the nation.

This steady growth of the wholesale must be thought of as a result. The cause was the steady expansion of local consumers' societies. It buys only for them, manufactures only for their needs. The central organization is their property and dedicated to their service. Across the counters of the retail stores moves an eighth of England's retail business. To an ever increasing degree the local societies are providing members with all the goods and service important for good human living. The movement started in a grocery store. It did not end there. The services which it provides now include food, clothing, furniture, automobiles, medicine, home construction, furniture, jewelry, fuel, drugs, credit, insurance, and even undertaking. In a slow, plodding fashion the consumers have been expanding their control over the means of production and distribution.

CHAPTER V

The Learned Can Be Wrong

THE LAST TWO CHAPTERS have been misleading. They have given the impression that the consumers' co-operative movement had a steady and unchecked growth—unattended by the usual problems and controversies which go along with the ordinary development of human institutions. Such certainly was not the case. During the first half-century it grew when even some of its friends questioned its right to a place in the sun. The movement owes a debt of gratitude to Robert Owen for effectively proclaiming the necessity of social control of machines. But it took fifty years for it to recover from Owen.

He glorified man's role as a producer. He sincerely hoped for the day when workers in factories would own them. It was inevitable that he should think in those terms. Back of him lay the centuries of hand production in which the men who produced owned their own tools. The shoemaker had been owner of his awl and last, the weaver his loom, the spinner his wheel, the smith his forge and anvil. Machine production made these hand tools relics. Those who worked with them became laborers in factories which other men owned. Owen wanted to restore the possession of the tools of production to those who were the producers. He saw that collective ownership of machines was necessary to this end. He wanted to substitute collective ownership of machines for the former private ownership of hand tools. This, for him, was the way to restore labor to its former dignity.

He attached some value to having the workers own their own stores but he had no large sympathy with grocery store co-operation. It was a good method of making a meager income go further— nothing more. It was just a penny-saving device. Producers' co-operation was the pure form. All other forms of collective enterprise were subordinate to it.

Most of the immediate followers of Owen shared his point of view. The Rochdale Pioneers probably accepted his general idea. There is evidence that they started with a store because they realized that it was all their meager resources made possible. They may have felt that the store would create savings sufficient to establish a producers' organization. The haste with which they rushed into the purchase of a flour mill with a producing capacity far beyond their immediate needs indicated their basic producer interest. It is, of course, impossible to determine accurately their motives and purposes. Their meager records—mostly minutes of their meetings—leave much to conjecture. It is difficult indeed to read the events of the past with the mind of the past.

The mantle of Robert Owen fell at his death upon a group known as the Christian Socialists. They were churchmen who shared his concern over the state of the nation but who did not share his antagonism to Christianity. Charles Kingsley and Thomas Hughes were the best known of their number. All were men of education and ability.

They were thoroughly enamored with Owen's idea about worker ownership. They, like him, preached it in season and out. Laborers should own the machines they tended and use the profits of production for mutual benefit. One of them states their point of view in these words: "Theoretically the idea we endeavored to spread was the conception of workers as brethren—of work as coming from a brotherhood of men associated for their common benefit—who therefore rejected any notion of competition with each other as inconsistent with the true form of society. And without formally preaching communism, we sought to form industrial establishments communistic in feeling, of which it should be the aim, while paying ordinary wages and interest . . . to apply the profits of the business in ways conducive to the common advantage of the body of those *whose work produced them.*"

When the magazine *The Co-operator* appeared in 1860 the Christian Socialists dominated its editorial policies. When the Co-operative Union was formed —a federation of societies organized for spreading

co-operative propaganda and for fighting the legis-
lative battles of the movement—the Christian Socialists were prominent in it. One of their number,
Vansittart Neale, was its executive secretary for
many years.

It is interesting to note that the intellectual leaders of the Union, whose membership was largely
made up of consumers' societies, were for half a
century men whose primary interest was in promoting another type of economic action.

Owen and his Christian disciples had an excellent
idea. There was only one thing wrong with it: it
wouldn't work. These men organized many societies
of producers. They invested capital in them; lauded
them as being the highest form of co-operation. But
such societies had a most disagreeable habit of failing. All the idealism of the Christian Socialists could
not keep such enterprises on an even keel. Workers'
co-operatives simply refused to stay solvent.

Faith has a strange habit of persisting in spite of
evidence. These men were not at all discouraged by
the failure of one after another of their pet schemes.
They were constantly at work promoting new ones
to replace those that expired.

The directors of the co-operative wholesale were,
during the early years, completely dominated by
Christian Socialist ideas. As a result the wholesale
subscribed time after time to stock in producers' organizations. Not a single voice was raised in protest

against such appropriations. The co-operators were all orthodox Owenites.

They did not all remain so, however. Deficits are hard to argue with. As the directors saw wholesale funds lost time after time, skepticism began to develop. Enthusiasm for investment in producers' co-operatives began to wane. As enthusiasm cooled, hot arguments appeared in the co-operative press. The board rooms of store societies rang with heated discussions.

Further fat was added to the flames when the C.W.S. started production on its own account. The Christian Socialists were very suspicious of this process. The organized consumers were invading a field which ought to be kept sacred for "pure" types of co-operatives. For the wholesale to take such action was in their eyes treason to the fundamental purposes of co-operation.

When it became apparent that the wholesale would persist in its heresy, schemes for having the workers share in profits and in management were brought forward. The wholesale directors tried and rejected them because they failed to work in practice. A divided managerial responsibility was simply impractical. With the abandonment of these schemes came louder protests from sincere men who believed that man, the worker, was more important than man, the consumer.

In 1874 there came to the presidency of the

wholesale a quiet man by the name of John T. W. Mitchell. He was the first to challenge seriously the dominant Owenite philosophy of some of his associates. He lacked all the advantages of formal education which some of his antagonists had enjoyed. He was born of obscure parentage in the back of a saloon. He received most of his schooling in a Congregational Sunday School of Rochdale. But he had native wit and the intelligence to grasp the basic facts of a situation. Co-operation was a passion with him —but a passion disciplined by a mind that refused to ignore results and the stubborn testimony of balance sheets. He defended the moral right of consumers to control their own affairs. He stood at the fore in many heated debates in congresses of the Co-operative Union and in conferences of C.W.S. directors.

The Christian Socialists, with the eloquence and the studied phrases of school-trained men, spoke of the sacred rights of labor. Mitchell took his stand on an ancient platform of Adam Smith, "Consumption is the sole end of all production: and the interest of the producer ought to be attended to only so far as it may be necessary for promoting that of the consumer." He insisted that consumers were the whole public, while workers were only a portion of the public. The interest of the whole ought to be set above the interest of a part.

Mitchell and his opponents were alike perfectly

sincere in their contentions but events fought the battle for him. The consumers' movement grew and got things done. The producers' associations consistently failed. Finally, when Mitchell was within three years of the end of an eventful, useful life, a new champion arose to defend his point of view—a woman, Beatrice Potter, who later became Mrs. Sidney Webb. In 1891 she published a book, *The Co-operative Movement in Great Britain,* which was simply a marshaling of the evidence. She laid to public view the record of the two types of organization: producers and consumers. Facts triumphed over the eloquence and persistent faith of the Christian Socialists. The dominant idea of Owen had run its course so far as the co-operative movement of Great Britain was concerned.

His basic conception was tried in the crucible of experience and found wanting. The co-operative store which he held to be of minor significance to the desires of the meek to become property owners proved itself to be all important.

With that controversy settled the co-operative movement became self-conscious. It had come to know its own power and to see its own purpose. Maturity replaced the strain and stress of adolescence. Time and energy, which had been spent in endless debate and in chasing after the unattainable, was now harnessed to an expanding program of economic conquest. Co-operation moved forward to its present place in the economic life of England. The nation whose inventors ushered mankind into a new economic era gave the world a business technique by which machines can be harnessed to the task of satisfying human hungers.

CHAPTER VI

Around the World

CONSUMERS' CO-OPERATION arose amid the social unrest which followed the wars of Napoleon. It was the child of the Industrial Revolution. It was the result of a search for a pattern of business organization which would properly distribute the riches machine production helped create. It came first in England because the Industrial Revolution began there.

However, it is not an English movement. As the modern techniques of production spread around the world the economic problems which it created spread with it. Out of the efforts to solve them came like results—consumers' co-operatives followed the spinning jenny, the power loom, the steam engine, when they went globe trotting. Scotland established her first Rochdale co-operative society in 1851. Denmark and Russia followed fifteen years later. Sweden tried in the sixties but couldn't make the idea work until the present century. Finland had a like experience. France had successful stores as early as 1885.

Iceland, Switzerland, Belgium, Hungary, Jugoslavia, Norway, Holland, Estonia, Lithuania, Bulgaria, Italy, Greece, Poland, Rumania, Spain,

Portugal, Argentina, Mexico, Australia, New Zealand, India, Japan, China, Palestine, Canada, South Africa, Turkey, Armenia, Egypt, and the United States all have important co-operative movements.

Some of these countries have made economic history. The story of Sweden's conquest of recurring depressions, of Finland's growing peace and security for the masses of her people has become good news in a world of gloom. Denmark has written a saga of heroic economic and cultural achievement. Hers is the tale of a small nation, defeated in war, with meager natural resources, rising to social greatness in a generation. In thirty-five years she revolutionized her business life, reduced farm tenancy from fifty per cent to five, and has made security and culture available to all her people.

Iceland is the most completely co-operative country in the world and she has the smallest percentage of illiteracy of any nation on the globe. In Belgium the movement has been an important factor in making it possible for her to support Europe's greatest density of population. The Swiss have used co-operation as a technique for making good living possible in a mountainous region. The common people of Russia have managed to build a powerful movement in spite of the opposition of the Tsars, war, revolution, and the excesses of her state socialism. Even saber-rattling Mussolini has bowed to economic realities and permitted the Italians to co-operate as consumers to provide themselves with food, shelter, and clothing.

Germany alone of the world's major countries has a prostrate movement. Naziism has thus far been definitely anti-co-operative in ideology and action. Only vestiges remain of her once powerful co-operatives. Time and time alone will tell as to whether studied hostility is a passing or permanent policy of the Third Reich.

All the countries mentioned have co-operative wholesales. Many have seen the consumers going far in manufacturing things for themselves.

The co-operators of the world are united in an international, interracial fellowship called the International Co-operative Alliance.

The idea of some such organization was germane with Robert Owen. In 1835 he founded an Association of All Classes of All Nations. By 1836 it had two hundred seven members—all residents of London. Owen defined the objective of the organization in the following terms: "The object of the association is to effect peaceably and by reason alone an entire change in the character and condition of mankind, by establishing over the world the principle and practice of the religion of charity for the convictions, feelings, and conduct of all individuals, without distinction of sex, class, sect, party, country, or color *combined with a well devised equitable and*

*natural system of united property ... for producing
and distributing in the best manner the best qualities
of all kinds of wealth abundantly for all."*

In 1837 he made a trip to Paris, Munich, and
Vienna to interest others in his idea. But Owen's
dream was a spirit without a body. By 1879, however, a sense of international co-operative fellowship
had begun to grow. When the national congress of
British societies was held at Whitsuntide, eighteen
persons from other countries were present. The
number included Dr. Edward Pfeiffer and Victor
Aime Huber, co-operative pioneers of Germany;
Professor Vigano, who initiated co-operation in
Italy; Rev. H. Christian Sonne, father of the Danish
development; Axel Krook, who tried in vain to interest the Swedes in the idea; and representatives
from Switzerland and Greece.

Further developments came in 1885. By that time
the number of societies in France had become suffi-
ciently large to make desirable the formation of a
national federation. E. de Boyne was one of the
guiding spirits in the French development. He had
organized a successful local society at Nîmes. He
nurtured the idea of forming the French Co-operative Union. When that organization was being born,
he invited representatives of the English societies to
come as fraternal delegates and give counsel and
encouragement. This invitation was gladly accepted.
The next year, 1886, de Boyne went to the English

congress and there proposed that an international union of co-operatives be formed.

The proposal bore no immediate fruit. For one thing de Boyne himself had no clear idea of the function of such an organization. In the address presenting the matter he talked vaguely about the need for an international organization to arbitrate the disputes between employers and employees which were making the industrial world a great battle-ground.

The International Alliance finally did get under way in 1895. The first congress was held in London beginning August 19. Earl Gray was the first chairman of this consumers' league of nations. French, Belgian, Dutch, Swiss, and Danish societies sent delegates. One American, L. O. Nelson, was present and was made a member of the provisional central committee.

The first years of the Alliance were marked by controversy. The fight between the Christian Socialists and John T. W. Mitchell in England was reflected in the international organization. In fact, the Christian Socialists took a leading part in creating the Alliance for the very purpose of using it as an instrument for furthering their ideas. It was their last battle line in the hopeless defense of producers' co-operation as the one right and exalted form of mutual aid. They asserted that only those business enterprises which shared earnings and management

with the laborers were true co-operatives and altogether righteous. In their opinion private businesses
which maintained schemes of profit-sharing with
labor were more to be desired than consumer-owned
enterprises that did not.

In accordance with this fixed and unshakable idea
they sent out a call in 1892 to both co-operatives and
interested individuals asking for an Alliance that
would support the profit-sharing scheme: "We propose that the alliance of which we invite formation,
shall not be confined to co-operative societies or their
members, but shall include all firms or companies
which accept the principle of the participation of the
worker in profit as part of their constitution or sys-
tematic practice, and all persons, whether heads of
industrial bodies or not, who signify their approval
of this principle by becoming members of the
alliance."

This proposal was toned down by 1895, but its
basic idea was foremost in the minds of many who
attended the first congress. In fact, the chairman,
Earl Gray, declared in his opening address, "The
question which will occupy our chief attention during
this week is the consideration of how we can best
promote in industrial enterprises the profit-sharing
principle."

The fight over profit-sharing was not alone responsible for making the early years of the Alliance
a period of strain and stress. Its loose membership

requirements aggravated matters. All kinds of organizations were admitted; consumers' societies, agricultural marketing associations, producers' co-operatives, and even profit-sharing private businesses. This made for a lack of common purpose and common philosophy. Individuals were allowed to become members on payment of a contribution to the budget. This brought in a lunatic fringe—men with pet ideas, who by joining the Alliance could buy an audience which they could obtain in no other way. Much of the talking in early congresses was done by the latter group.

Gradually, however, the growing power of the consumers' societies made itself felt. The individual memberships were abolished and voting placed on a delegate representative basis. The continued failure of worker-owned co-operative production societies in England slowly silenced the advocates of profit-sharing. Leaders of consumers' co-operatives were perfecting a philosophy which gave moral justification for a procedure which had shown itself to be sound in practice.

Matters came to a head in 1904 at the congress of the Alliance held in Budapest. Hans Müller of the Swiss Co-operative Union closed an address on "The Organization of Consumers' Societies in Rural and Semi-rural Districts" with these words: "Co-operation is an economic and social movement for liberty, which, by means of the organized building up of a new order of the economic and social conditions on which our existence depends, aims at obtaining both for the individual and the people at large, a great amount of independence. Therefore, whoever sincerely desires to promote the co-operative movement in any respect whatever must never forget to banish the old state of dependency and to be most careful never to replace it by any similar institution."

A debate followed in which Dr. Müller asserted his firm belief that the end and goal of co-operation was the abolition of the dependence of the common people upon the institutions of capitalism for the goods necessary for abundant human living. Its design and purpose was the building of a new social order in which the exploitation and inefficiencies of capitalism were no more.

Conservatives were alarmed by such sentiments, but the Congress, as a whole, saw in Dr. Müller's statement only a logical and clear-cut presentation of the basic purpose of the movement.

Not only did this congress declare it the purpose of co-operatives to free the consumers from their dependence on capitalism; it also asserted that co-operatives should keep themselves free from dependence upon the state: asking and accepting no subsidies or loans from government. Representatives of agricultural marketing associations were offended

75

at this, for they loved to have their organizations sustained by public funds.

The total result was the loss of some members. The marketing association dropped out of the picture as did some of the more conservative consumers' groups—particularly the German. But the next few years saw the ranks filled with new organizations having the philosophy of such leaders as Hans Müller. Unity of purpose replaced the divisions of the first years. Definiteness and decision took hold of the Alliance. It had achieved maturity. From 1904 on it has been a consumers' Internationale dedicated to giving the common man better access to food, shelter, and clothing.

Today forty countries are represented in the membership of the International Co-operative Alliance. Over 193,000 local societies having more than 65,000,000 shareholding members are included in its great fellowship.

The Alliance is a people's league of nations. It is not controlled by diplomats representing imperialistic and warring governments but by those who see in collective activity as consumers a means of achieving a better human society. Instead of plotting and counter-plotting in contests for position and power, the delegates at its congresses plan ways and means for making mutual aid more effective in economic processes. The needs of the common man are the same the world over. The basic hungers for food and clothing, for adequate shelter, and some of the beauties and luxuries which make civilized living possible, are present in every race and nationality.

When it began, the Alliance was primarily a fellowship of like-minded people who met for the purpose of swapping ideas and experiences. But now the tie of common ownership of the means of production and distribution is giving torso and limbs to its spirit of brotherhood. International co-operative wholesaling has become a reality.

The English and Scottish Wholesales own their tea plantations in India and Ceylon together. Danes, Finlanders, Swedes, and Norwegians are served by an international wholesale society with headquarters at Copenhagen. This organization is binding the consumers of all four countries into a closer and closer unity. The successful "Luma" electric light bulb factory is their common property.

The Alliance has assisted in the creation of an International Co-operative Wholesale Society which is actively engaged in promoting trade between the co-operatives of various countries. It began operations in 1924. The volume of its business steadily increases. It is now more than $20,000,000 per annum. Committees are at work preparing for an international co-operative bank and an international insurance society.

CHAPTER VII

In Nineteenth Century America

THE FACTORY SYSTEM which so seriously disturbed the social and business life of England came to America very soon after it had gotten under way in the mother country. In 1789 a mechanic named Samuel Slater came to the New World bringing with him a first hand knowledge of the production methods developed by Hargreaves, Arkwright, and Watt. He bore neither blueprints nor drawings, for it was a criminal offense for anyone to carry out of England sketches or models of machinery. He carried his plans and models in his head.

He built the first American mill at Pawtucket, Rhode Island, completing it on December 21, 1790. Sixteen years later he and a brother constructed large factories near Slaterville in the same state. By 1810 the United States had over one hundred manufacturing plants in operation, all of them erected according to Slater models.

Thus machine production was smuggled into America.

Its arrival brought suffering to American labor as it had to the English working men. Long hours, low wages, child labor became the rule. The writings of Seth Luther and James Montgomery, first American students of labor problems, bear witness. They report that working days were from twelve to fifteen hours in length; wages sixty-five to seventy cents. Sometimes the lash was used to stimulate production; not infrequently deductions were made from wages to support churches which pious employers required their employees to attend. In 1831 fifty-eight per cent of the factory workers of the industrial East were women and seven per cent children under twelve years of age.

Against such conditions men revolted. A few intellectuals became apostles of Robert Owen. He came to America in 1824 to preach his doctrines and establish a co-operative village at New Harmony, Indiana. His preachments moved some of the finest spirits in America to take up the battle for better conditions. Horace Mann began his great fight for free education. The Rev. George Ripley established the famous Brook Farm Colony in 1841 which was an attempt to show the way to Utopia. The followers of Charles Fourier dotted the country with Phalanxes—operating on the principles of Owen's co-operative villages and failing as consistently.

The working people themselves created trade unions and political parties to fight for a ten-hour day and better wages. Strikes were by no means infrequent. Most of this agitation got nowhere against an indifferent public opinion. The population of America was predominantly rural and the farmers saw no sense in the demand for a ten-hour day. Clergymen preached against it on the grounds that men should be contented with their wages and on behalf of the glory of work and the dangers of idleness. Manufacturers opposed it for obvious reasons.

One of the numerous labor organizations born previous to the American Civil War was the New England Workingmen's Association, organized in Brahmin Boston in 1844. It was this group which first saw the possibilities of laborers bettering themselves by working together as consumers.

Shortly after its organization John Kaulback, a tailor, brought forward the suggestion that interest and attendance at meetings would be stimulated if the members formed a buying club, raised a little capital, and bought household necessities together. This was done. Substantial savings were made over regular store prices.

The membership soon became so engrossed in the co-operative buying program that it overshadowed all other purposes of the Association. In 1845 a store was established as a means "of bettering the condition of the working class."

The management was instructed to sell at prices which would defray the actual costs of operations and pay a maximum of six per cent on invested capital. Business was to be done for cash. Persons not of "good moral character" or users of intoxicants were not permitted to own shares.

The move seemed timely. The store flourished. By 1847 twelve groups of people were operating businesses on these principles. They banded themselves together in what was called the Workingmen's Protective Union. Two years later the name was changed to New England Protective Union. By 1850, 106 local Unions were operating stores. The 83 whose records are known reported a combined capital of $72,000, a membership of 5,100, and sales totaling $650,000. In 1852, 167 reported a combined capital of $241,000 and sales of $1,696,000.

The next year internal difficulties arose to plague the movement. The stores did much of their buying through the central purchasing agency in Boston, of which John Kaulback was manager. The agency was controlled by a "Board of Trade" on which the local Unions were represented. Certain groups were dissatisfied with Kaulback and persuaded the board of trade to discharge him. His friends resented this. They withdrew from the New England Protective Union and organized a rival organization called the American Protective Union.

The new organization soon outgrew its parent. Four years after the split it boasted 327 local societies whose total investment of $290,000 supported an annual trade of $2,000,000. The 327 stores were scattered in some ten different states.

The New England Union had 63 active stores whose total capital and sales were about half those of its rival.

1857 was high tide for the movement. In thirteen years over 700 local stores had been set up. Many failed, but most of them were able to liquidate in an orderly manner with their affairs in reasonable condition. Some 400 were carrying on what seemed a successful program of merchandising.

1858 brought its conclusive evidence of decline. A few months of uncertain prices upset the calculations of managers and directors, discouraged the faint-hearted, and led directly to many liquidations. Competing business had learned to adjust its prices to Protective Union levels. This wiped out most of the apparent advantages to the consumers and caused many to lose interest. Finally the shadows of a great war diverted the attention of men and women from their bread and butter problems. Unit at a time, the movement waned.

When the war was over, a few stores remained in existence. By 1890 only three were left: one at Natick, one at Worcester, in Massachusetts, and one at Salmon Falls, New Hampshire.

America's first great consumers' co-operative effort failed. It was inevitably so. The Protective Union had no precedents to guide it. Its leaders made a stab in the dark. The story of the Rochdale Pioneers was an untold tale. The saving device of avoiding price wars by charging market prices and paying refunds to the consumers was then an obscure English invention.

The Protective Unions were quite like the Union Shops promoted by Dr. King. They operated much like them and failed through similar mistakes. They did survive longer and grew larger. America did better with her first attempt at establishing consumer-owned stores than did England. Unfortunately, such cannot be said for later efforts.

The first Rochdale co-operative established on American soil was located at Lawrence, Massachusetts. It began operations in 1863 on a capital of $1,400. It flourished for a few years, but eventually died.

The second extensive wave of consumers' co-operative activity came after the war. It was a child of the inevitable post-war depression. When the tragic conflict between the North and South was over it left the economics of the nation out of joint. The vanquished territory had been ravished. The northern states had an overexpanded industry geared to the destructive needs of Mars.

When the soldiers were mustered out of the armies they went home to a northern labor market, already glutted, or to a devastated and impoverished southern agriculture. In an effort to start life anew many of them set their faces westward to take homesteads on the virgin acres of Iowa, Minnesota, the

Dakotas, Kansas, Nebraska, and Oklahoma. They were joined in this move by unemployed industrial workers and by a wave of immigrants who swept into the United States as soon as the war was over.

Rich land fertilized by human toil yielded bumper crops. The agricultural production of the nation swept to a new high and the prices of farm products hit a toboggan. Those who had worked hard to give the world more food were rewarded for their effort with privation and in many cases loss of their land. Many a homesteader had borrowed at high rates of interest to get his stake in the world only to find himself closed out when the land became his, because he could not pay his debts. The sheriffs' hammers beat a tattoo up and down the American frontier.

Hardship fell not on the pioneers alone. The farmers of New England and the other eastern states found it hard to compete with the more fertile and productive western lands. They shared in the general agricultural depression.

Against these hardships the farmers rebelled. They resented the fact that often the railroads got more for hauling produce to market than the producer received for all his work. They claimed it was unjust to have to pay debts incurred when wheat sold for more than a dollar a bushel with grain worth half its former price. They felt it was unfair for manufacturers to keep up their prices amid the general suffering.

So when Oliver Hudson Kelley, founder of the great agricultural fraternity, "The Patrons of Husbandry" or Grange, went out to organize the farmers of America he found them ready and waiting. The Granger movement became prairie fire.

This secret order was the direct result of Kelley's concern over the post-war conditions among farmers. Shortly after the war he had been sent out by the national government to study conditions. He found them so disheartening that he resolved to set up an organization to give farmers a greater sense of the dignity of their profession and to make them more skillful as tillers of the soil.

The first local or "subordinate" Grange was established in 1868 at Fredonia, New York. Others followed in Minnesota, Wisconsin, Ohio, Indiana, Illinois, Iowa, Kansas. During the early seventies Granges were chartered by the hundreds. By January 1, 1875, the United States had over 21,000 of them acting as rally centers for embittered and embattled farmers.

In 1869 the Minnesota State Grange took action to establish a state exchange to assist subordinates in the buying and selling of goods. News of this step spread rapidly. Soon the Grangers' resentment against their treatment in the market place expressed itself in programs of co-operative buying and selling. The selling program never advanced very far but it wasn't long until co-operative purchasing was a part of the activities of nearly every local group.

There was no uniformity to their plan of operations. Some established stores financed through the sale of shares to members, a great many more appointed local purchasing agents who pooled orders for supplies, bought them at wholesale, and passed them on to the consumers at a small margin of profit. In a few cases, particularly in Illinois, the Grange at first stayed out of the commodity business and encouraged its membership to join with other groups in the establishment of stores to serve all the rural population.

The business program aroused great enthusiasm. The farmers believed that it was to be salvation in the midst of their pressing difficulties. The interest is reflected in the cold figures of Grange business records. Iowa led the field with a volume of $5,000,000 in 1873; Indiana did a wholesale business alone which exceeded $300,000 in 1875; the Ohio State Grange purchased over $100,000 worth of groceries from one wholesale house in 1878; the Maryland warehouse handled goods whose value totaled $358,000 in 1877. Just one of the joint ventures in Illinois did a $100,000 business in 1873. This was the largest in the state but several others were in existence during the first half of the seventies.

After an almost phenomenal initial success with its business program the Grange began to have a sharp decline in membership. The root cause was weaknesses in the commercial activities. The National Grange gave no guidance to the farmers' desire to co-operate until 1875. Each local and state organization did about what was right in its own eyes. What seemed right was usually wrong. This was particularly true with the price policy. The whole initial emphasis was on saving money. It was a natural emphasis for a people in serious plight financially but it was a fatal one.

Where stores were established it got them involved in price wars which they could ill afford. Where the business agent system was maintained prices were often put so low that they did not cover the actual cost of doing business. This resulted in false conceptions of value which sometimes had weird effects. In 1878 the Ohio business agent complained because local Granges objected to a one and one-half per cent commission necessary to make the wholesale program break even.

The results of these policies began to make themselves felt in 1874. The first state to feel them was Iowa. Her state Grange launched a farm machinery factory which promptly went into bankruptcy. This brought on the virtual collapse of the Granger movement in the state. Other states followed in short order.

The peak of membership was January 1875. At that time there were over 21,000 local bodies of the order. A year and one-half later the number had shrunk to a bare 15,000.

Much of this decline might have been avoided had the National Grange concerned itself with the commercial program earlier. But it was not until 1875 that a sound plan of co-operation was brought forward. During the year previous the national officials had made contact with the English co-operators, mastered the Rochdale plan, and come to believe in it implicitly. The 1875 national convention of the order endorsed it. Following this action pamphlets were printed and distributed asking local Granges to adopt the English practices. Every effort was made to reorganize the consumers' co-operative program on a sound basis.

In 1876 the national body went even further. It approved a plan for covering this country with Grange-sponsored Rochdale co-operative societies, the establishment of a national wholesale to supply them with goods, and the creation of an Anglo-American co-operative exchange to serve both the English Co-operative Wholesale Society and the proposed Grange wholesale.

Thus for the first time in American history a comprehensive program for establishing the consumers' co-operative movement was approved by a great farmers' organization. But the plan never